FLASHBACK TO THE...

AWESOME '80s

By Patty Michaels

Illustrations by Sarah Rebar

Ready-to-Read

SIMON SPOTLIGHT
An imprint of Simon & Schuster Children's Publishing Division
New York London Toronto Sydney New Delhi
1230 Avenue of the Americas, New York, New York 10020
This Simon Spotlight edition May 2023
Text copyright © 2023 by Simon & Schuster, Inc.
Illustrations copyright © 2023 by Sarah Rebar • Stock photos by iStock
SIMON SPOTLIGHT, READY-TO-READ, and colophon are registered trademarks of Simon & Schuster, Inc.
For information about special discounts for bulk purchases, please contact Simon & Schuster Special Sales at 1-866-506-1949
or business@simonandschuster.com.
Manufactured in the United States of America 0323 LAK
2 4 6 8 10 9 7 5 3 1
Library of Congress Cataloging-in-Publication Data
Names: Michaels, Patty, author. | Rebar, Sarah, illustrator.
Title: Flashback to the ... awesome 80s! / by Patty Michaels ; illustrations by Sarah Rebar.
Other titles: Flashback to the ... awesome 1980s! Description: Simon Spotlight edition. | New York : Simon Spotlight, 2023. | Series: Flashback to the . . . | Contents:
Totally Trendy! — Far-Out Fashion and Fads — Say What? | Audience: Ages 5 to 7 | Audience: Grades K-1 | Summary: "In the 1980s, boom boxes and breakdancing
were all the rage. Cabbage Patch Kids were flying off the shelves, and a new TV station called MTV was launched. Kids will love learning about the first at-home video
game consoles, jelly shoes, leg warmers, eighties slang, and VCRs! Lighthearted illustrations and approachable language introduce young readers to all this and more
hallmarks of the awesome decade"—Provided by publisher. Identifiers: LCCN 2022040419 (print) | LCCN 2022040420 (ebook) | ISBN 9781665933469 (pbk) | ISBN
9781665933476 (hc) | ISBN 9781665933483 (ebook) Subjects: LCSH: Nineteen eighties—Juvenile literature. Classification: LCC D848 .M525 2023 (print) | LCC D848
(ebook) | DDC 909.82/8—dc23/eng/20220826
LC record available at https://lccn.loc.gov/2022040419
LC ebook record available at https://lccn.loc.gov/2022040420

GLOSSARY

Answering machine: A machine that receives phone calls and lets callers leave a message at the beep

Boom box: A large, portable music player

Camcorder: A combination video and audio recording device

Cordless phone: A wireless, portable phone that receives signals from a station connected to a landline

Floppy disk: A square plastic disk where data from a computer is stored

Gnarly: A slang word for excellent

Mullet: A hairstyle where the hair is short in the front and sides, and long in the back

Perm: A chemical treatment that gives your hair permanent waves or curls

Rad: Another word for cool

Tubular: A word meaning awesome or excellent

VCR (videocassette recorder): An electronic device that plays videocassettes and can also record content from your TV onto them

Walkman: A small, portable music player that can be listened to with headphones. The Sony Walkman was one of the most popular brands of these kinds of music players in the 1980s.

Note to readers: Some of these words may have more than one definition. The definitions above match how these words are used in this book.

CONTENTS

Chapter 1
Totally Trendy!

Let's go traveling back in time,
way back . . . to the awesome 1980s!

Get ready for a totally **tubular** ride as you learn about trends, fads, and other **rad** things that helped define the decade!

Some of the most popular toys were Teddy Ruxpin, Transformers, Rubik's Cube, Cabbage Patch Kids, Simon, and Strawberry Shortcake.

By 1983 almost three million Cabbage Patch Kids had already been adopted!

In addition to playing with these rad toys, kids in the 1980s were also busy with **gnarly** activities like roller-skating, skateboarding, and playing video games at an arcade.

But with the rise of at-home
video gaming systems, kids started
spending less time at arcades.

Gaming systems like Atari, Nintendo, and Sega Genesis let kids play popular games like Pac-Man, Donkey Kong, Tetris, and Frogger right at home!

The famous inventor and co-founder of Apple, Steve Jobs, once designed video games for Atari, earning five dollars an hour!

When kids weren't playing video games, you might find them listening to music.

You could hear lots of pop and rock songs on the radio, and new genres like rap and hip-hop were becoming bigger and bigger.

The music channel MTV premiered on August 1, 1981, bringing music videos to homes all over the country!

Music in the '80s was best listened to through headphones plugged into a portable cassette player, like the Sony **Walkman**.

Or, even better, you could blast your favorite songs out of a giant **boom box**!

Anyone who grew up in the '80s will remember making homemade mixed cassette tapes by recording songs off the radio.

(And can you believe that back then you had to actually rewind cassette tapes by pressing a button on your radio or stereo?)

You could also manually rewind a cassette tape by using a pen or pencil, *if* you had the time.

TV was pretty different in the '80s too. There weren't nearly as many stations as there are today, and there was definitely no streaming or on-demand viewing.

Many TVs back then didn't come with a remote control, so you had to manually change the channel!

Saturday was *the* best day for kids to watch television. It meant Saturday-morning cartoons! Kids would grab bowls of their favorite cereal and plop in front of the TV to watch popular shows like *The Smurfs*, *Jem and the Holograms*, *He-Man and the Masters of the Universe*, and *Teenage Mutant Ninja Turtles*.

If you wanted to watch your favorite show, you had to watch it at the time it aired.

Luckily, **VCR**s became popular in the 1980s. If you set your timer, you could tape the show and watch it later.

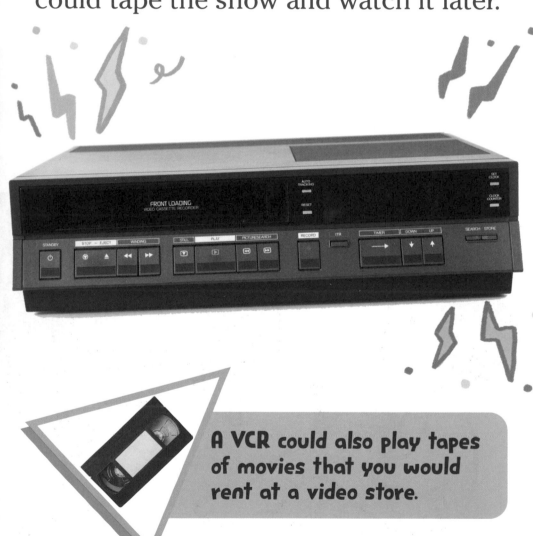

A VCR could also play tapes of movies that you would rent at a video store.

Home **camcorders** became popular too. Since digital photos and videos didn't exist yet, this was a great way for families to record their memories!

Chapter 2
Far-Out Fashion and Fads

When it comes to fashion and style, the 1980s were, like, the coolest decade ever.

Popular hairstyles included **perms**, side ponytails, and teased and crimped hair.

Another popular hairstyle was the **mullet**. It was described as "business in the front, party in the back"!

Neon colors, layered looks with tutus,
tracksuits, bomber jackets,
and leather jackets were some
of the hippest looks of the decade.

Accessories like jelly shoes, scrunchies, fingerless gloves, charm bracelets, giant hair bows, bucket hats, and oversized gold chains were super trendy.
(And some of these trends are once again popular today!)

Jelly shoes became all the rage in America after their debut at the 1982 World's Fair in Knoxville, Tennessee—and the rest is history!

Chapter 3
Say What?

Methods of communication in the 1980s were *way* different than they are today. Take phones, for example.

The days of a phone only connected to a wire were coming to an end. People were psyched to talk on **cordless phones** and leave a message on an **answering machine**.

Alexander Graham Bell was awarded the first patent for an electric telephone in March 1876.

Telephones also looked really fun in the 1980s.
Some were shaped like cartoon characters or foods.
You could even see through some phones!

One of the first cell phones hit stores in 1984. Nicknamed "The Brick," it weighed almost two pounds!

Computers were also very different in the 1980s.

They were large and heavy, and you saved information on a **floppy disk**.

And as far as the internet goes?
That was *years* away from being
readily available in people's homes!

The GIF image format was invented in 1987, but the engineer who invented it meant for the word to be pronounced "jiff"!

Owning your own computer
was rare during this decade
since they were very expensive.
But you could always go to your local
library to use one.

Did you know the first
computer mouse was actually
made of wood?

Typewriters and word processor machines were much more common and affordable.

Back then a word processor was the actual hardware that helped with writing and editing information, not the software programs still used today to create documents, like Microsoft Word.

Did you have fun on your awesome time-traveling adventure? Weren't the '80s super awesome?

Now that you know a little about what was popular in the 1980s, can you name some things from that decade that are similar today? What things are completely different?

Make Your Own 1980s Time Capsule!

Now that you're an expert on all things from this awesome decade, here's a fun activity that you and a grown-up can do together! Ask them what they remember about the 1980s and if they have any souvenirs they can give you (like a ticket stub, jewelry, or a photo). Then either draw or print out pictures of things that you learned about the decade. Place all of your collected items and pictures in a large plastic jar to create your very own 1980s time capsule that you can display in your room!